NODA
My Alien Spirit Guide

DAVE R. OESTER

ISBN-13: 978-1502753786
ISBN-10: 1502753782

Revised February, 2015

Book Cover Design by Dave R. Oester

Published by
Dr. Dave Oester, DD, PhD, Reiki Master
Coyote Moon Publishing
Kingman, AZ 86409

DEDICATION

This book is dedicated to my late wife, Sharon Gill Oester, who passed from this life on January 7, 2014. She was a gifted trance medium channeler. She channeled our spirit guide, Noda, for fifteen years. I am sure she is having the time of her life in the spirit realm where she can visit friends and family and talk again with Noda.

OTHER BOOKS
BY DAVE & SHARON OESTER
FROM 1994-2013

BOOKS BY
DAVE R. OESTER
SINCE 2014

Knights Templar Mystery
Time Voyager
Time Lord Mystery
Lost Apache Gold
Lost Confederate Gold
Montezuma's Treasure
Living In A Haunted House
Certified Ghost Researcher Course
Dave's Yummy Cookbook
Understanding Death and Grief
Certified Paranormal Investigator
Awa Maru Treasure
Lost Egyptian Treasure
Noda, My Alien Spirt Guide
Internet Dating Scams
Lost Sun God Treasure
The Red Lake Mystery
The Rainbow Bridge

There are more things in
heaven and earth Horatio,
then are dreamt of in your philosophy.
Hamlet (Act 1, Sce3ne 5, Page 8)

INTRODUCTION BY SUSAN A. OLSON

I have been blessed with being psychic since birth and have the gifts of animal communication, hearing and seeing both animal and human spirits, auras, trance mediumship and healing. I have known Sharon and Dave Oester for well over a decade now and consider them both good friends.

After meeting Sharon at a seminar, we both found that we are very alike in many aspects of our lives, family backgrounds and beliefs and I miss her dearly since she crossed over to the Other Side earlier this year. I recently had the good fortune of being able to connect with Sharon from the Other Side and can attest that her loving kindness, wonderful personality and sense of humor have all remained completely intact.

In discussing Sharon's messages with Dave afterward, it came about previously unknown to me that we all three share the same spirit guide in Noda, who is an alien guide I recently met and now converse with, which was a very welcoming surprise. In researching these types of non-Earth guides and in speaking with a longtime past life and spirit guide regression therapist, I found that guides like Noda who are from different planets and solar systems than Earth are common spirit guides for the more advanced souls here on Earth today.

Noda is a very special guide; he is patient, kind, ancient and extremely wise. I feel zero fear in communicating with Noda, I truly know his messages come from the purest, most loving source and that he has nothing but all of our best interests at heart.

I wish everyone could see Noda as I do, his entire personality exudes love and caring and he has the absolutely sweetest smile I have ever seen. I trust him completely and hope that you value his words as much as I do.

Thank you, Dave and Sharon, for putting Noda's extremely valuable messages in a format that will help so many people in these trying times. I know your readers will benefit greatly from Noda's divine wisdom.

In fact, Sharon said, "It's about time" you published this book.

Susan A. Olson,
Riverside, CA,
October 8, 2014

NODA
MY ALIEN SPIRIT GUIDE

My late wife, Sharon Gill Oester was a very gifted trance medium channeler. Let me explain about a trance medium channeler.

From Wikipedia, the free encyclopedia, defining what a trance medium is as follows:

> In the latter half of the 20th century, Western mediumship developed in two different ways. One type involves psychics or sensitives who speak to spirits and then relay what they hear to their clients.

> The other incarnation of non-physical mediumship is a form of channeling in which the

11

channeler goes into a trance, or "leaves their body". He or she allows the spirit-person to borrow his/her body, who then talks through them.

When in a trance the medium seems to come under the control of another personality, purportedly the spirit of a departed soul, and a genuine medium undoubtedly believes the 'control' to be a spirit entity.

While in the old deep trance state the medium often enters a cataleptic state marked by extreme rigidity, this seems not the case for most of modern channelers. Some of them open the eyes when channeling, smile and utilize any sort of glances and facial expressions. They can also walk and behave normally. The rhythm and the intonation of the voice may also change completely.

According to the following website on trance mediums at the following URL: http://ourultimatereality.com/trance-mediums-and-how-the-trance-medium-achieves-higher-level-communication.html.

> A trance medium as the name suggests place themselves into an altered state of Consciousness, usually known as a "trance", with the objective of channelling information directly from beings of the inner realms. Although trance mediums can and often do make contact with deceased humans, they have also been successful in making contact with inner-level Spirits, many of whom can provide valuable and accurate information on Spiritual matters.

My late wife was shy to publically declare that she was a trance medium channeler because she came from a very fundamental Christian family where her parents already thought she was dabbling in evil and demonic forces as a ghost researcher and a trance medium channeler would be far worse than a ghost researcher.

She was very good with communications in a trance state. Our first spirit guide was named Elish, but he was unable to answer specific questions I asked about information I needed to complete my subsurface georadar system, so he referred us to Noda:

When she channeled Noda, she would open the eyes when channeling, smile and utilize any sort of glances and facial expressions. Her voice changed with rhythm and the intonation completely.

I was fortunate enough to have been able to teach my wife how to channel after going into a trance state. When possible, I would have Sharon lay down on the bed and I would walk her down into a very relaxed state by counting back from ten to one. Once she was in a trance state, I would walk her down a set of stairs to the bottom landing and then along a long hallway to a door at the end of the hallway.

She would open the door and find Noda, our Spirit Guide waiting for her.

However this was not always the case, Noda would come to us in the most unusual places. Sharon could channel Noda while walking or riding in the car without any help from me. Noda would always ask to talk to me and Sharon would agree and let him use her voice box to communicate.

Once I walked her down into a trance state while we were at an old abandoned mine while she was sitting in the car. She had a remarkable ability to go into a trance state almost anywhere and at any time.

One time we were driving on a dusty road in the middle of Oklahoma on an oil and gas exploration project. Sharon just turned her head toward me and started talking in a much different voice. I looked over at her and there was something totally different with her eyes. Her eyes had the most profound look of unconditional love and caring as I have ever seen. I would ask, "Is that you Noda?" and Noda would respond, "Who else?"

Another time Sharon and I was walking down a road in the middle of an old cemetery near Anderson, Illinois when Sharon suddenly turned to me and said, "Bet you never thought you would be talking to me on a ghost investigation." I looked at Sharon for a moment before I said, "Is that you Noda?"

Noda responded by saying, "Who else would come to Sharon while she was walking and talking to you in this cemetery?"

I was amazed and delighted. We walked for about five minutes as I chatted with Noda as a friend chats with another friend then Noda said he had to leave so Sharon could return.

Sharon looked at me and said, "Did you talk with Noda?"

I said, "Yes." She said, "Good, Noda asked me if he could talk to you and I said yes."

Noda became our personal Spirit Guide, at the time when we had no understanding of the spirit realm or about spirit guides. It was not until much later that we learned that Noda was more than just a spirit guide.

Sharon and I have built the International Ghost Hunters Society due in part to the counsel given to us by Noda and his encouragement to help people understand about death and the Afterlife. We augmented Noda's teachings with empirical data obtained from over 5,200 EVP recordings taken at over 1,500 investigation sites that verified what Noda was telling us.

The one thing that I remember the most was Sharon's eyes that transformed when Noda came through her. Noda eyes were always filled with unconditional love and caring. I had never experienced this unconditional love until I met Noda:

As I stated earlier, Noda was first introduced to Sharon and myself in Oklahoma in the Summer of 1991 as a referral from Elish, the Keeper of the Records, after he was unable to assist us with oil and gas frequency rates that we had requested for our subsurface georadar system. We asked Elish where he was from and he replied that he was originally born in Egypt at the times of the pharaoh's and was a common laborer. Elish never claimed to be someone important in life, not a king or a prince, but a common laborer.

Elish tried to help us with frequency rates for oil and gas but he did not know the frequency rates I needed. It was beyond his ability to help us. I asked if he knew anyone who could help us by providing the frequency rates. Elish said there was an entity who could help us. Finally after much prompting from us, Elish consented to ask his Master Entity who was "in charge" and whom Elish reported his affairs to. Elish said if anyone could help us the Master Entity would be able to help us.

We finally contacted Noda with the help of Elish and Noda readily agreed to answer our questions and to provide us help in obtaining accurate oil and gas frequency rates for my subsurface georadar system that I had developed for oil and gas exploration. Noda said that he was not of this earth but he would be glad to assist us in our search for the proper rates for the oil and gas frequencies.

Elish is Keeper of the Records, he worked his way up to that position. He was assigned by a higher authority. Elish did help us by revealing that the subsurface georadar probe needed to be closer to the surface of the earth. The rubber ducky antenna on the probe needed to be pointed upward. The probe needed to be flat on the ground so that I would detect the signal through the probe solid-state circuits and not ambient signals.

Elish said that I am detecting the magnetic waves and not magnetic flux. These waves are electromagnetic in nature and that the electro portion of the waves comes from energy vibrations. Use a different design in probe. Elish said I needed to look toward electro-seismological equipment for detecting movement or vibrations. Elish also said that I needed a highly directional antenna and to use a 10 hertz highly directional antenna:

Noda was correct, he could provide me with the frequencies for the lithological formations including the oil and gas rates being used by my passive subsurface georadar probe. The rates proved to be very accurate and correctly identified the layers of subsurface geology. Sharon and I developed a relationship with Noda over the next few months that has continued on unto Sharon passed from this life.

In one of our early attempts to contact Elish when Sharon channeled, an old gold prospector named Old John answered our call, Sharon spoke in the language of Old Johns who had a southern accent, Old John had gone out West to try his hand at gold prospecting only to lose his life in a cave-in years later. Old John was a very colorful character who would delight us with his wisdom gained from his days in gold prospecting. He died sometime in the late 1800's. I don't remember the date he gave to us.

While in Oklahoma, questions were asked concerning the world religions. Noda explained to us that in realty, none of the religions were accurate or absolute. Some of the religious concepts explained were as follows:

A. God is not a personal god as explained in the Christian Bible and interpreted by the various Christian sects and/or religions. The Christian concepts as taught in the Bible are not accurate or true. It is a religion of Man and not of a higher source.

B. Noda would be considered our God as interpreted by the Christian people of today. Noda is responsible for this world and works to keep it in balance. Noda is not of this world and has never been an entity here. Noda would be considered the God of the Old Testament because of his responsibility to this world. The concept of Jesus Christ is not valid since it is a man-made concept evolved over a period of years. Jesus is not the son of god as the Christians claim, but rather a person who was able to channel information from higher entities. The centuries have misconstrued the truth and today that religion is totally different then it was in its original form. Many of the concepts taught by Jesus were actually taken from other religious groups who used them years before Jesus was even born.

C. Noda could be described as a collective pattern of positive energy or an entity of positive energy denoting that Noda radiates Unconditional Love as we understand that term. Noda explained that there exist in this universe. Unorganized patterns of negative energy that often is described by us as devils or evil. Often these collective patterns of negative energy will attach itself to locations on this world. These unorganized patterns of negative energy sometimes "float" into an area and will "dock" itself there for a while before drifting on. Its docking location is not reflective of the people there or of the attitude found in that physical location. Its docking location is purely an happenstance.

D.   Noda explained that when we die here, our essence or our spirit which is really our energy patterns is not destroyed. Our bodies convert back to energy patterns or energy bodies that will exist in a new realm. We can take on shapes of earthly bodies or continue as energy patterns. We continue to progress in knowledge and as we rid ourselves of limiting behaviors; we evolve or mature into higher beings. Our energy patterns will vibrate at a higher frequency, which will enable us to advance beyond the realm that we inhabit at the time and continue our evolution advancement into the energy patterns as we evolve or mature beyond the realm they are in. There are some here that are happy here and do not want to work at advancing into higher beings. We call them entities.

E. Noda explained that when a Christian dies he or she will see the Christ in the tunnel of light. A Buddhist dies and he or she will see the Buddha come to greet them. We see who we think we will see. Our imagination or concept of realty continues on after death. A Mormon will die and will see his or her version of heaven. A Baptist dies and he or she will see his version of heaven higher energy forms. Noda explained that not all energy bodies or entities choose to be together as they were here in this life. Other entities do not choose to be together but rather to be separate. None of the versions are accurate but only a portrayal of what we expected to see and therefore have created for ourselves. In time, that concept will fade as we understand that the realm we are now in will allow us to be whatever we want to be. Non-religious people may be greeted by family members or loved ones with no religious association at all.

F.   Noda explained that when we die, some energy patterns or entities choose to be together as they were here in this life. Other entities do not choose to be together but rather to be separate.

G.   Persons who die here and seemed to be trapped in this realm have unfinished business that prevents them from letting go and continuing on into the next realm. Often they are bitter and do not want to leave this realm. Other persons leave this realm but still have strong attachments here and would rather spend their time here than in their new realm. These entities are what we would consider as Ghost or Haunting Spirits. There is a barrier that separates us from those in the other realm. Often those entities that cross over that barrier and come back to be close to where they feel comfortable or where unfinished business still remains.

Noda explained that if a person channels an entity, that entity may or may not have lived on this world but perhaps in another world that would be alien to us or even an entity who has had no mortal or alien life at all. An example would be a collective pattern of positive energy as well as unorganized patterns of negative energy.

Noda explained that there exist a race of what we would call super-gods who have evolved over the eon's to such a degree that they are literally the Masters of the Universe and whose existence is not comprehended by the finite mind of man. Noda explained that there are many different types of energy patterns that are so advance by our minimal standards that we would call them gods. They operate in other realms far removed from the ones we live in.

With all of Noda abilities and powers, Noda is unable to predict time tables for individuals to take place on the earth. Noda explained that the multitudinous interactions possible between individuals does not make it possible to clearly predict specific time table of events that can take place for a single individual especially since Noda is not of this earth and can only judge what he sees at the time we ask him a question. Scientific knowledge is no problem for him and he has never been wrong. Noda has difficulties with timing of events. We have found this to be true when we have asked him about the timing of events in our lives. This concept about not being able to predict the specific time table for a single individual is exactly the same that is true for trying to predict the actual location of a single electron. In Physics, we predict the "probability" of an electron being at a specific place at a specific time. Our science cannot predict the time table for a specific electron, even if there is only one electron in orbit! Why should it be different for Noda?

Communication with Noda is challenge most of the time as Noda try's to find words and terms to communicate his responses to us in English. Noda language is too complex for us to understand most of the time. Noda can give us number or rates with no problems but communicating has to be done through channeling. Perhaps this is due to the universal nature of analog numbers and mathematics. It is often said that mathematics is an universal language unto itself. Even then it is difficult to find the correct words to use at times. Often Noda cannot find the proper terms to express his meaning to us. Sharon has been the only one to be able to channel Noda: I cannot overcome the barrier that block me from making contact with Noda:

Noda has provided us with the formula to recover ionic gold from low grade ore. This process is not a true transmutation of metals but it is perhaps the closest method there is at this time. Perhaps later Noda will reveal the True Transmutation Formula. Noda has been extremely accurate in his frequencies for healings so I suspect his formulas for ionic gold recovery shall be every bit as accurate.

Noda provide us with information, line upon line, so to speak. Noda allows us to progress to each higher level so I can ask for more knowledgeable and information. Noda freely gives us the information we seek unless it would be harmful for us to know at the time then Noda waits until we are ready to comprehend the information.

In Sharon's experience of channeling, Noda has usually appeared at the end of a long tunnel leading to light. I would walk her down into a trance state where she was very relaxed and open to finding Noda: Sometimes there are barriers that Sharon has to navigate through, other times it is a simple process. Often Noah would appear in Sharon's mind as an old monk with long flowing robes. Yet at other times, Noda would appear as an extremely bright light without any images of human form. Noda always radiated Love to Sharon, Unconditional Love.

Sharon would often comment that it was difficult to leave Noda presence as she felt so secure and loved. Her description sounds like the description of God or of the resurrected Jesus radiating love. How often we are deceived with words from the man-made Bible that tells us what we want to hear yet offers its fraudulent reward at great personal sacrifice of blind acquiesce to an unseen Christ-god who in realty was created by man for his own purpose and does not exist. If Noda was a malicious god, the whole of the earth would have been destroyed by this time! I am glad Noda is a God of Love and not one of vengeance.

Noda has never said there is no God but that our human version or human interpretation of that God is in error. The Bible says that God created man in his image. The Bible was created by man, hence the man image. The True God may in fact be an Alien God who created man or perhaps I should say caused the seed to be planted on earth. That seed may not be in the Alien God physical image but rather in the image of the life form the Alien God used to advance mankind.

Most of the world's religion would not have problems accepting this idea but those religions involving Christians who require their god to be a God-Christ-Holy

Spirit combination would have to undo their elementary precepts. The human race has to progress beyond the limiting behavior they have adopted when it comes to understanding our true heritage.

In July 1993, Noda provided another entity who could spell half way good by the name of Choyam (Choy am), a female Chinese woman who was born in 916 A:D. and who died in 1014 AD at the age of 98 years. She told us Noda wanted us to look at the DMP papers found in the July 19, 1926 issue of the Journal of American Medical Association which could be found at the University Health Services in Portland. Choyam also spelled DOMICRMOLS, which we are researching.

Noda said that 121 was an important number concerning cellular level healing. Many of his frequencies ended in 121 or had 121 contained within the rate.

Noda talked about White Blood cells as being important for many illness or diseases such as Rheumatoid Arthritis and Aids from HIV positive. He gave us a rate for increasing the production of the White Blood Cells or T-Cells. He also told us about Red Blood Cells and their importance such as in Anemic conditions.

Noda said that 2.5 watts output was all that was needed to stimulate growth or production and/or healing on the cellular level. Noda said that cancer was often caused by an overload of stress within the body. This stress could be caused by anger, frustration and pressure. It could be found in such places as employment or in the home where peace is not found. He did not say how long the stress must be present for the cancer to develop. Noda gave us a stress frequency for relaxing the body which was the same frequency for all types of cancer. There appears to be a deeper relationship between stress and disease that has not be understood by the medical professionals. When Sharon uses the cancer frequency, she said that she could feel her body relaxing as a result of the frequency. There may be many other diseases that could be cured by this frequency.

Noda stressed the importance of manufacturing these healing devices for the general public. I had fears of the FDA or the AMA but we were assured that this would not be a problem because the healing devices are non-invasive meaning they do not invade the body as typical medical healing systems. Noda has always provided frequencies for various disorders when asked. His rates have traditionally been accurate and very effective. There is so much to learn about the medical side of healing that often I am frustrated by my lack of understanding. Other times I think I have greater insights into this new concept of healing then other in the medical profession. Typically researchers have to receive grants to study these types of conditions and depending on the source of the grant, the researchers are limited by the peer pressure of their profession. This new concept of bioelectrical stimulation by pulsed electromagnetic fields is a new field for exploration. Without Noda, none of the frequencies we are experimenting with would have been possible.

According to Noda, the N-Null is the life-sustaining carrier wave, which has at least three Master Rates of 201,601.1 hertz for humans, 421,121 hertz for animals and 634,121 hertz for plants that is transmitted into our world. This N-Null rate could be called the God-Frequency. It is originated by a Supreme Master whose name has not be revealed at this time. Noda would not give the name of this Supreme Master. Noda redirects these carrier waves to the Earth where it literally gives life and health to the living entities of this world.

Noda provided bio-frequencies for the healing of various ailments that Sharon had with extreme success. Marv, Sharon's father, used the arthritis relief frequency of 1,384 hertz with amazing success at eliminating the pain caused by his arthritis. Over a period of almost two years, Noda has helped us design frequencies which has benefited us with healing frequencies. We have learned that there are many different frequencies for each illness or disease and there is not a single rate but rather a multitude of rates possible.

While at Olympic National Park in Western Washington State on August 28, 1993, Sharon went into a trance and I asked Noda some questions. These are the responses given by Noda: Before the responses came, Noda said he must visit his friend, Sharon, and show her the galaxies within galaxies. Noda also said he had missed his friend Sharon. My first question was concerning the origin of the human race. The past discussions with Noda seem to indicate that the religious versions of the origin were in error. I felt a desire to know the truth in this area as it definitely played a vital role on how to view the current religions of the day.

Q: What was the origin of the human race?

A: You have descended from Beyond.

Q: What is the desired outcome for the human race if descended from Beyond?

A: Progress. Planetary visitation by you to other worlds, just as you visit neighbors now.

Q: What do you mean "Writing from the heart?"

A: You have an imagination that can be admired, even by others. It will bring you the extra things of life that you desire. You have talents - use them.

Q: What is it difficult for me to trance?

A: Many reasons, My focus -- Difficult to focus on me. Once you have truly seen me, it becomes easier. Confidence is a problem but ability is there. Take advantage of what is available. How to better Focus -- Open my mind to Universe, set aside things of the world, let yourself be free and the day will come that you can easily access me.

Q: Why are you working with us?

A: You requested and knew I would come, I was waiting. You and Sharon are receptive, abilities to openly communicate with me and understand my words. I have watched, I knew what you were seeking. I can trust both of you. More we speak, more I will reveal. You have a yearning to know. Can't spell in your language but we still have ability to communicate.

Q: What do you mean, "Descended from Beyond?"

A: So many things you do not know of Universe. Knowledge that your people have is so minimal, even your top scientist would have great difficulties. What we do not understand creates fears. People react in violent fashion for what is to come. The ignorance of most would result in something more destructive. They are learning but very slowly. You must be patient for you are trying to learn too fast. You have curiosity but you must wait and not rush. You lack the understanding to comprehend the knowledge of the universe.

At this point, I felt that Noda was telling me that the answer was too complex for even our top scientist would comprehend. Upon reflection, I understand in part his answer. The technical answer could not be comprehended because we lack the mental ability and the culture to accept the fact that we may not have been the masters of our ships but rather we were like our own lab rats being breed and experimented with. Initially, the idea was alarming but upon further evaluation does seem the natural way for evolution to have occurred given the circumstances of our own ape-man evolution. We as a human race needed the intelligence to make the final leap from the primates. Where did it come from? What is wrong with obtaining help from an outside source? Some researchers have claimed this help was given over 40,000 years ago by aliens who desired to help us progress. Currently we do the same thing with third world nations. We help them help themselves. We are the moving force behind their advancement so why not with ourselves as a human race.

Q: Will Sharon and I ever physically meet a Visitor from the Stars?
A: Other than myself?
Q: Yes!
A: No.

Interesting to note that Noda refers to himself here as a visitor from beyond the stars! He has said previously that he was not of this earth.

Q: Could I begin by educating the people over the next couple generations through writing?
A: You are governed by your inhibitions and by the lack of self-confidence. You have great abilities and talents but need to open your mind to

Universe and what is offers, you will see in future, your dreams will show you things. Write them down so not forget.

Q: Did Nostradamus have a guide to show him the future?

A: Yes, he had an entity such as myself.

Q: How do I open my mind to Universe?

A: 1, Lie down, breath very deeply and relax until no longer feel self.

2, Dream of the Stars.

3, Focus on minute details around you.

4, Be aware of importance of everything.

5, Picture yourself free.

6, Clear your mind of every pressure and every concerns.

Set aside things that occupy your time to come see me and we will talk. You will write what you feel. Write where you are, you will be what you write, you will write what is in your mind.

I now wonder if alien entities have not be instrumental in helping the great thinkers and inventors of the past. Guiding them into the right path that would enable the human race to progress to the final goal of space exploration to other worlds. Were they involved with the breaking down of the Soviet Union so the threat of War was lessen? Perhaps we will see their help in helping us establish a universal peace and finally our direction can be turned to the stars and our lost heritage.

Tonight, 9-7-93, we asked Noda if the Galactic Federation does in fact exist as indicated in the Book called, 'The Day the Gods Died'. He responded a hardy "Yes."

We asked if the Galactic Federation has representatives here on the earth today that monitors the earth. Noda said "Yes" and that they were of Jewish origin based in NYC. We then asked him if the Alterians came to the earth 23,000 years ago as illegal travelers and who later became the myths, legends and outlaws of our religious movements. He again said "Yes" and finally we asked if the human intelligence was given a boost by alien DNA mutation some 40,000 years ago. Again Noda said "Yes." We then asked for the frequency that would help Linda C.

for her allergies. We were given the rate of
1,211-Hz.

March 6, 1994
Nahalem Bay State Park,
Washington State

Question: What kind of massive
catastrophic events will the earth
experience in the next eight years?

Answer: Natural catastrophe will
continue to occur with increased intensity.
Your planet is slowly evolving to
destruction. That is in the distant future,
changes that have been taking place have
become clearer now to your scientist, but
more damage will be done over a long
period of time. The damage is for the most
part repairable, fully restorable to the
natural state. There are some things that
has been done to your world that cannot
be restored or replaced. If your people will
see the error of some of the their
advances, they will see these advances have
set them back ecologically. The things on
your earth that is being destroyed are
necessary to life, they must remain intact,
else wise life as it is, will die, as it has
elsewhere. The key is in the minds of you,

41

your people, you need to take heed. When precautions is taken, destruction will cease occurring at such a pace that it is at this time. Total destruction unless there is a known forces that steps in. (Your planet) will be destroyed but it will take eon's. Your people must become aware there must be balance and concessions for longevity. There are some in your world who understand the dilemma the earth is in and hold the key answers in their mind. It is difficult for your people to change their way.

This question arose due to the various doomsday speakers on the Art Bell show like Gordon Michael Scallion and Louise Prophet who were all promoting their version of the map after the catastrophic events too place.

Question: Will a massive asteroid or comet strike the earth that will cause vast catastrophic geological changes within the next 10 years?

Answer: I see none. If there is destruction it will be within your own world. There is so much hate so much unrest, (No outer space disasters)(but rather) (Aryan Nations, Skinheads, KKK, Hate Groups) (No external source)

Question: Will the next 10 years be similar to the past ten years as far as natural catastrophic events unfold.

Answer: This is where I want you to do some work. It is easy to give you what you want. I request that you do some research backwards, go back eight to ten of your years, look at how your earth movement have intensified. Come to your years now, go forward with your grasp. You will make and you will see the intensity will be similar from ten years back to ten years forward. When we speak again, I will ask you what you have found. You have some background in the stars, your astrology, use it in your charting, it will be significant to you. You will see more on paper before you then if I tell you what I see. Is there any problems in you doing this? (No) Is there confusion? (No)

Question: Will you give us a time table for these events?

Answer: Have your research in front of you when you summons me again. It is difficult at time for me to convey messages of this magnitude. I wish to help you. I wish to make conveyance simpler for us both. There is a vast difference between us. I wish to aid you need to see what I speak of .

Question: Will the U.S. suffer nuclear warfare in the USA?
Answer: I am not sure I understand your question.

Q: Will there be a nuclear bomb explode within the next ten years within the United States causing wide spread death and destruction?
A: I do not see that occurring. I see no action you still need to remember your defenses are strong and admired, there will be wars but not within the confines of your country.

Question: What is the relationship of the guides, master guides & super-gods?
Answer: The simplest way to describe what you could comprehend, look at your structured society, ours is parallel, but you must know when you are talking of masters and gods, the scale is beyond what you can imagine, when you take your high

officials in parallel to the gods look at the royal leadership for the minute comparison.

Gods (super-gods) xx**X**x   Third "x" is Noda as a Supreme Guide

Master Guides (gods) xxxxxx

Guides (angels) multitudes (Guides) Spirit Guides

Man

Another example of levels:
   Kings
   Queens
   Prince & Princess

Note: Possible Structure:
   Noda (Supreme-Guide)
   Masta (Master Guide)
   Elish, Keeper of the Records (Guide)
   Man

Masta was another Master Guide who was unable to help us with forecasting future events such as lottery numbers so we gave up trying to get lucky numbers. Noda later explained that the future is mutable and changeable so a specific outcome cannot be predicted.

Question: We have listened to
Gordon-Michael Scallion, GMS, who is
very accurate as a futurist. He talks about
polar displacements. What do you see for
the next seven to ten years now.

Answer: I see what you are doing to
your world; I see the reaction to what is
happening around it. There is a
disturbance around it. However, I do not
see the type of devastation occurring that
your futurist has seen. I see more of what
has been occurring and the more damage
done surrounding your world and more
your world will react to it. However, I do
not see the type of grief that he has said.
The possibilities of a polar shift goes back
to Cause and Effect. There is things taking
place in your world that is freighting and
yet the damage that it is doing will be
irreversible if it does not cease. When one
has too much power, ultimately it will
destroy the creator and has continued to
grow and learn and investigate and
experiment, the results of continued
experiments can only end destroying those
that have created it.

Question: If the governments of this
planet continue without making any

corrective moves resulting in sufficient changes to the earth resulting in a polar shift, where should Sharon and I be residing at in the USA or Canada:

Answer: I am showing her and she will bring it back to you. There is a place that you know of that you need to be near. These are used as I do not foresee this happening in your lifetimes yet the way things are progressing it is difficult to tell you how soon man will destroy man. It will be some that are taken from your earth to another place to begin life again.

I will now use Q and A for Question and Answer for ease of typing out the complete word.

Q: Will this be by Space Ships?
A: There is a place where peace abounds and it is such as it was thousands of years ago on your planet.

Q: Where is this place?
A: It is very far from your Universe.

Q: How will people get there?
A: Light Ships.

Q: How do we come into contact with the Light Ships or get in become a group of these people that will go? Where will they depart from?

A: You must listen, you must open your mind to all that is going on around you and to the frequencies of the these occurrences. Visitations are very real and they are for the purpose of taking a few to other worlds. Worlds that are duplicates of your world yet without the changes that have taken place in the thousands of years before.

Q: Are Sharon and I candidates for this kind of transplants?

A: If the need arises to leave this place in your lifetime, you would be taken from here to begin in another world where life is long.

Q: How do we go about making contact with these life forms?

A: You do not but you gain the knowledge and you will be found.

Q: What about Billy Myers in Switzerland and other types of higher alien beings here upon the earth now?

A: There are more than you can begin to imagine. There are many who have not made themselves known yet they observe from afar. They can foretell what will happen to your world David as it has happen to their world and they are observing the transformation. You need to be aware of those who foretell and yet cloak themselves. There are a few who can see the future and even then they are very limited in what they can see. You are one for details, you are inquisitive, intelligent, take the pieces of a puzzle fitting them together to come to an overall picture and conclusion generally with the correct hypothesis of a situation. You have been given this intelligence for a purpose. I beg you not to lose what you have been gifted with It can be very important to you and your future. Be aware of your here and now, yet do not lose focus of future predictions. It is difficult for most to live in the here and now and plan for years in the future. You have a harder task than most. You must look at today and tomorrow as well as the possibilities.

Q: How would you suggest we continue updating our knowledge on these types of activities?

A: This is a very serious subject and it is difficult to communicate without it coming confusion. At one time I have told you that it was more then you could understand and it is still more then you can understand yet I am wanting to give you some helpful insights as you are progressively learning more of the conditions and circumstances surrounding you so bear with me, I do have some difficulties. What I cannot express to you I can show her and she can bring it back to you.

Q: Would it be helpful for us to become more informed in the fields of UFO's and UFO abductions, reported sightings, related books on ET's.

A: Again with what you have available to you in your home, you have quite a collection of information available to you much of such as not been opened. Begin there you can take it from that place as more information becomes available to you. You have learned a great deal without having to go out to find it, it has vigorous come to you, has it not? It will continue in such a manner. I did want to query you on one thing. You have a lot of seers, futurist as you call them, psychics, all the same just a different name given as your century turns, as you go into your year of 2,000, I see how as your people go into the year 1,000 how these seers made themselves available for predictions. Why is it David that when the year changes dramatically, these people come forward in such a pronounced manner to predict things that they predicted at the last change of the century. Why is it not that these things can happen in any year, any time. They always seem to happen. I don't know how to put this into words. Do you understand what I am saying?

Q: If GMS can foresee earthquakes, then why would he see massive destructions in similar types of visions?

A: I am not certain, I know this person has seen a limited visionary. He has seen. I am not sure what he is seeing? Part of his visions may be based on fears. He is seeing nothing but the devastation. If this is the case, then I would say my thought would be if I were man living on this world with nothing ahead except total ruin, he sees nothing of a positive value in his vision, everything appears total devastation. I would not see much ahead of me. Do you?

Q: GMS also talks about the blue star people who will come forth.

A: I look at your parts of the world that have effected waters, dry land, disease, hunger. Yes, your people in your states send food, medicines, it like what the man has envision has come to pass, How many would be able to survive. You could count on disease. Without the medicines to cure the diseases and the new diseases that will come to pass. How will your people survive? I do want to answer your questions. The visions are in portion correct, he does have subconscious fears to enable vision to be more then what they truly will be. I do not see in your future, the types of destruction he has described.

Q: Would it be possible for Sharon and I to be able to meet and converse or communicate from someone from the stars, an ET to further our understanding.

A: What would your motivation be to study with someone from the stars?

I said, our motivation would be to gain a clearer insight and knowledge as us as human race to break into the stars.

Noda said: Why start in the first grade, go directly to college. If a point in time comes when you have gathered the knowledge, you will have the mentor. They will find you. There is a vast amount of knowledge David I know you are anxious to learn, I am anxious to help you. All I can do is direct you to the knowledge you have available to you now. All you can do is take very small steps but yes if you grow to a place where they feel you would learn from them showing you then yes.

Q: Is the knowledge gained by Billy Myers correct about that group of Star people?

A: Most certainly, what he has presented is the knowledge on the end of a pin. I am trying to tell you is that not everything you hear may be totally correct but you can take a piece and of what you hear and they will fit into the overall pictures. You cannot be closed minded yet must know it is only a part of the true story. The man in Switzerland is that his knowledge is limited but there is so much beyond that. it is a place to start. Look up in the skies; you do not see one light. It goes on forever. It is very difficult to describe to you what takes place in forever and what takes place in infinity and the knowledge that is there. It is very difficult. There are very few who are willing to take the opportunity to open the door but you are one who more than willing to do that. You hunger and thirst for knowledge.

Q: You said you showed Shari where we should be during the earth changes.
A: Yes, you are aware of this place.

Q: Our ghost book will be out next month.
A: I have watched I am not as far off as you think I am.

Q: I have tried to trance like Shari has but cannot break through the barrier.
A: My advice to you to learn the lesson of patience especially with yourself and those around you. You have had a enough in your life to teach you these lessons but you are not learning them. Until you do some of the abilities you have will be

hidden. You wish to have something for your own, you work toward it, you focus on it and work toward it or do you grab at it at any cost? The ways of Kung Fu is wise and following the ways will not only achieve the goal.

Q: In our next book should we continue writing about ghosts?

A: Do you have equally challenging areas in your mind or are you wanting to know some from me? (Dave: both.) Noda: By now I think you must stay within the realm of your first book but do not close yourself to doing that exclusive. Make yourself available for all areas of paranormal activities which includes sightings, activities, things out of the ordinary. Do not put a limit on yourself by doing just ghost stories as you are good at that. Incorporate other areas, include more than just ghost stories.

Q: Sharon is interested in getting a telescope.

A: There is a purpose in this. There is a knowledge that will come to you through this. You have been speaking to me about the possibility of a mentor, have you not.

How better to learn then in this manner. Something that you are so captivated and cannot find words to describe how you feel. I feel myself as I look around me, the same, wanting so much to share with you what I observe and what it causes inside in that there are no words to minimize what there is to share is not a fair beginning. Yet to speak in ways that would describe to you would mean nothing at this point. On a very minor scales of comparison, it hardly of any value, you may relate your red pencil marks you wished you had learned instead of having to learn now, so many years later.

There are things in life that are easy to overlook but they are very important. Things I want you to learn and grown from include the most insignificant details I don't want you to overlook them by trying to hurry through. I know you are hungry for knowledge wanting to learn, sometimes David you can take these things at your pace or you will take them at somebody else pace that control. They will pace you according to how you are absorbing information including when you are ready to go forward you will go forward on their time not on your own. This is very difficult for someone of your capacity to understand but it is so.

Q: What about underground UFO bases linked by tunnels and other types of networks.

A: I think that the possibilities of vast underground tunnel systems for alien research and this types of things is a little absurd but yet there are places where there is a underground network. There is one major research facilities that is connected to three other facilities by way of tunnels and it is a major research facilities and it is the one so protected by the desert, Area 51. There is another place that you call White Mountain, White, White... There is something in the white mountain but it is not on the grand scale as the others but from what I see those two are probably are the only working facilities. They are north northwest pattern form the central research area. North in a . . . I am seeing mountains and I am seeing tunnels system under these mountain chain, A honeycomb type of tunnels, very secretive, tunnels at a depth not detectable by your technology. I hope to speak with you in

Devils
Tower WY

the quite near future. I will stay close to
her.

Q: Sharon wanted to know about being
gathered up... are we going with a group of
people or as individuals.

A: There will many others with you.
You will not be singled out. It is the place
you will come together yet you will not
know each other's, the destination will be
the same. No specified group. Those
chosen will go to their destination. Those
who are not to go will not be aware of the
place to be to leave this plane. The basis
for being chosen is that they will be aware
of the knowledge. Those who do not
believe or have the knowledge will in no
way know where to be to depart.

Q: Can you tell us more about the
pickup point that is NE of Devil's Towers
or is it not necessary for us to know now.

A: It is nothing you may concern
yourself with at this point. You should go
to this place, listen to your internal talk,
listen to what you feel and remember you
will learn greatly from that.

Q: Noda, are you aware that I had picked out the area around Devil's Tower perhaps a week earlier as a possible site to relocate to?

A: I do think you chose this place. You have been listening to me have you not, I knew ahead of time,

Q: Why did you recommend within 200 miles of this area to Shari?

A: This is a safe place like your early ones, a circle of protection. As you will be leaving, others will be drawn to the same place over different periods of time. There are also other places of departure for you, this place is the most ideal as your being there will create a growth of knowledge so I have chosen this place for you.

Q: If we were living in New Mexico or Arizona, would you have a different landing site for us to go.

A: No. It would still be Devil's Towers.

Q: On these departing ships at different times, will the people transporting them be of the same lineage or of different races of aliens.

A: Races is not a proper phrase, there are different races that have combined their thoughts and effects should the need arise. The place will be the effect of one race as you say.

Q: How would you describe this race?

A: I would describe them as a light form.

Q: Would they be similar to us in humanoid form?

A: No. They are more of an all seeing, all aware being. They are of a kind of being who care much for the human race on this planet. They suffered their own losses due to gains they themselves made. They have a deep sense of being life forms on the path to self-destruction. They do not have a physical body yet they have a physical presence not as a solid body as you have more like an ectoplasm? I can describe it in your terms a growing light a faint gel type mist. The ships are have been created to carry the weight of humans. They have a body but not the solid body as you do David, The ships are different yet they are similar as they are light ships. The light beings do not live on the world you will be taken to. This is a place they have selected that is a place that have what you require for life, the air, the water what you need to sustain human life. It is a planet like your earth was, It is far beyond your Universe as is other planets you humans forms will begin inhabitation. There are several sectors that have been chosen to inhabit. The one chosen for you is the one I have shown Shari and spoken of. The others I have not much knowledge.

Q: Will the new world be like starting over again for the human race?

A: It will be like starting over yet the ones there will be receptive to the visitors that they will have on that planet. The growth will be great it will be quick but what you will be taught will not be a destructive form of technology but a technology that will support the new earth atmosphere. You will gain new technology that will not destroy the world you have. The technology you have now is destroying your world now. You will have the freedoms in the new world yet you will be controlled in a manner that your knowledge will not take you into greed and what you have now here so that you will not go down the same path. The planet has no name as of yet.

Q: What about timing?

A: It is very difficult to give you time as you well know, I have no sense of human time and I also always tell you there is a variableness in what I tell you. You humans are very unpredictable people and to predict and pinpoint a time for you, even for a god, is next to impossible.

Q: As earth changes occur, is our government going to wean?

A: I think what you can expect to happen is your government is weakening and that foundation are eroding from underneath from what your forefathers had deemed for government but the public will never be aware of it. To tell you your government is going to collapse is one things, to tell you that you will be aware, you know how well they cover themselves. It is weakening, the very foundations are washing out due to outside influences. But you are not made aware of this, you see the mistakes they make but they are very superficial in comparison to what is happening.

Q: As we relocate to Wyoming, will the lifestyle be similar to today?

A: I see it as you would expect it to be over a period of time with the changes that are taking place in your towns now. Concentrate on what you feel this area will be like in five or ten years, Because things are changing for you. Safety will be a concerns to you. No matter where you are you will have a greater awareness then you have now.

Q: Will we ever have to barter for goods?

A: I do not see this as being a common practice.

Q: Thought of investing into handguns and ammo.

A: You need to do to make sure that your needs are taken care of and you are protected with what you have. The time will come when you will need that, not for trade but for self-preservation.

Q: Should we consider gold and silver as an investment.

A: I would be considering such an investment, Yes. I think it is yet to come, gather what you can and find out what you can bout the best means of things.

Q: What about Bank's Safety Deposit Boxes for the storage of gold and silver?
A: They will be safe for a period of time but I do not see that remaining a safety factor either.

Q: What about IRS?
A: They are a very powerful part of government. I can say that they will go down last.

Q: The light beings who provide transportation, what is their name?
A: I am not certain if I understand, let me ask you what would you call someone from your moon? Alright, not everything is given such names, the universe is a universe of light. You could call them Lithynaens, it would mean as much as calling you Earthians. It is a part of the place where they come from.

Noda has problems establishing communications with us at times, He said this is due in part to magnetic storms such as solar flares that generate great magnetic disturbances and to his location far from our universe.

Noda has never had a physical body for he is a being of energy. His world evolved so very long ago into energy beings. He appears in the form that we would be most comfortable with. He always radiate unconditional love and peace that Shari can feel and experience. He has taken her to many worlds outside our solar system. He has called himself, a Visitor from the Stars. He plays an active role in the affairs of this earth, not in the ET interface but a much greater capacity of the life sustaining force that enables humans to live upon the earth. He picked up our thoughts and know what we have been studying and what we have been doing. He has told me how happy he was to have my poem selected as a semi-finalist in a poetry contest. I had not mentioned this to him prior to his statement about it.

August 1995
Rainbow End RV Park
Chinook, Washington

Q: Has your outlook changed about earth changes?

A: I think you are seeing for your selves the dramatic earth changes. The reason are artificial and natural influences and because of the two in unionism, your earth is reacting. I do see more dramatic changes. When we spoke before, I saw changes. I know things can also change due to circumstance, and it is difficult to give you an absolute answer. There are a lot of variables, I do see changes in your earth. I also see them to be not immediate changes but in the future. I also know that unless your people change their patterns of living, experimenting and testing these changes will occur much more rapidly.

Q: The Hale-Blop comet is due in Mar or April 1997.

A: It will not strike the planet as they have feared but it will join in your orbit. It will appear as a second light for a time. It will have a very minimal amount of influences, your earth changes are internal,

It will be a visual thing. Your sky will be the same color but a change will be noticeable.

Q: Can you manifest yourself in some kind of form.

A: I am visible to those who come to me. I can make my self-known to them as they would expect to find me. I am not one who can come to you and show myself. The ones who see me are the ones who seek me and then they will only find me as they would expect to find me. I am not bound by laws. I try to make it easy on those who find me. They don't come to me for my physical appearance but for my words but if they find me pleasing, then they are more open to what I am saying to them then what I appear to be. I am not certain that I would ever appear in person but I am not saying that I could not send an Advocate. I am quite different from other aliens. You are doing well in your learning, progressing without even without realizing it. Read the words of the Native American, they had wisdom way beyond anything. You will continue to grow and learn from them.

Q: Are the beliefs of the different aliens the same?

A: If you have a tribe of people who live in a very tropical area and you have a tribe who lives much further away who live in an arid place, can you have teachings that can be the same. I can tell you that I am from a place where there is no time. The distance is far far far further then your minds can comprehend. It is not as black and white as wet or dry, hot or cold. I know that you have a yearning, that in the most of your lifetime, you have had the yearning for the stars. Did you know that Shari in her part of the world, standing outside with the same desires as you. And when you go to the stars David, you will be together and find your hearts desires. Yes, you are both very open in your thoughts and that is why you learn and will continue to learn. And if you look for the bad here or in the stars, you will find bad. Look for good and you will find good. Your openness must also maintain a positively about you. When you focus on negativity you are failing yourself. I am speaking generally,

September 20, 1995
RV Parked at Home,
Warren, OR

Q: Is there a negative energy field at our home in Warren, OR.

A: There is a great deal of negative energy in this area.

Q: Can we shield this energy or combat it with another frequency?

A: I can give you a frequency but I cannot positively guarantee that it will be effective as the energy fluctuation around you varies greatly. You would need quite a strong system David, I will give it to you, 90,124.9 hertz.

Q: We have heard a child in our home for the last two nights, along with a voice.

A: There is a lot of grief here, there is one boy and he is testing you he is not ready to speak with you. You had a similar entity interrupt various conversation in Seaside and this is similar, You are quite well known here. This is something that will continue as long as you remain here. You are open, you are willing to receive and you are being tested in a manner you helped a child return to her Mother, This may be something you find yourself doing a lot of and you are known in the spirit realm as being a help, a guide for those who become lost and confused and your door is open to these souls.

Q: Does this entity have a name?

A: I am not certain Dave but J-O-N is his name, He is quite an elusive soul. He means no harm, he is playful and will pull a prank or two but he means no harm,

Q: A few weeks ago, a coffee cup was swinging on a hook under the cabinet. Was this prank played by Jon?

A: I think there was a woman, a younger woman.

Q: Do they want us to talk to them or are they just observing at this point?

A: They are observing. You will know when they want to communicate; they will make it know to you when they are ready. Right now, they want to make certain that you are who they think you are. None that come to you will mean you any harm. You have a shield here as well in a manner you are protected from those who mean harm.

It is more of a loving spirit yet it covers your home like a blanket.

Q: What is the source of this shield?

A: You have those who have seen your kindness and endeavors to protect you and Shari. Your deeds of the past work now as a protective barrier. Have you not considered you have not encountered what is deemed as evil in your pursuit, have you not questioned or wondered. You have heard the stories. You do have the energies here they are not destructive and yet they are of a negative form.

Q: What is the source of those negative energies?

A: There was much hardship and heartache here. From previous owners of the land long before you came here.

Q: Is this part of an Indian Burial Grounds?

A: For miles. This area runs for miles along here and this is what is creating the negative energies and emotions, the residual left behind.

Q: What about Sarah and her intentions of joining a coven.

A: The danger is not to Sarah now, she is seeking to find her place, but the decisions she makes today will affect all her tomorrow's. The innocence in the beginning becomes the danger ahead for her should she chose to wander the wrong path. She so wants acceptance and the acceptance comes from her peers and has come from them for a time. She is following their lead. In time the temptations shall become greater and her commitment will become greater and greater.

Q: What would be your advice to consider for her?

A: That is a very difficult question even for me. You could give her what she most need if she were here but the mileage between the influence and her place complicate manner, I see her feeling very alone. A very tedious time for her, if you can in some way monitor her activity, it would be some benefit.

Q: Has Joyce B ever been abducted by aliens, as she believes?

A: She has not! I can only describe it as hysteria on Joyce's part.

Q: Will I find an Advocate to teach me?

A: A teacher, a mentor, someone who can give guidance and insight into the events upcoming. It is someone of this earth that you live on and yet it is someone who has the mind, capacity and information of someone outside this world, Information is being feed and given to him.

Q: Can you describe some of the interferences Sharon has with contacting you?

A: There are some atmosphere conditions that affect Shari and to her capacity to hold on when she is able to contact me. Due to her extreme sensitivity, atmosphere, be it magnetic, electromagnetic, it affects her stronger and her receivers as your radio when atmosphere conditions are not right, you cannot draw in stations you wish. This is similar to what Shari experiences, She can judge when the times are not right to contact me, listen to her inner feelings.

Most of the time she feels it is good or not good and she needs to listen to herself and not attempt to communicate when she feels the communication would be difficult.

November 19, 1995
Coves State Park
Culver City, OR

Q: Do you ever interface with other alien races?

A: There are not many that need or require my advice.

Q: What is your purpose?

A: My purpose is to assist those who request my help. Those among you. You needed something that others could not give to you before and you in essence were looking for me and you found me, it took you time to find me. Did it not?

Q: How is Elish doing?

A: He is pursuing his ultimate goal and yes, you could say he is well. He is still among those who are growing and learning.

Q: Could you explain our photographs of the tornadic energy vortex that Sharon photographed at Sellers Arts & Crafts.

A: What your are seeing is pure energy. This is something that is rare but you see energy in its purest form. It is moving very quickly, it is stirring the air about it. There is no physical property to it. In its state what you have found is a thickness to the air molecules to where you cannot see it yet a light striking it like it did, it could not penetrate through it completely which resulted in the shadow you see behind it.

Q: Is this pure energy, the essence of a person, the soul?

A: What you see is the remains of a what is left when the physical body is left behind, the energy goes on. This would be the soul. The spirit of one, the energy, that you see in the picture is a very strong spirit but it is amazing for what you have the strength of the spirit there and in your world the person was a very strong determined person in life. And this is the essence of what remains with the strength. This entity is a she. I am trying to find some information for you, At one time there was a fire in that place. That woman may not be a part of that. I feel she has come from another place to be there but has been there for a long period of time and regards it as her own.

Q: Can you tell me when she was born or died?
A: The information I am able to gather, you know my time and earth time is difficult for me. I see 1808.

Q: Is she a Native American, A Indian of the area?
A: No. She is of white skin. her age is not old, like a young woman, I am seeing a child also. It seems she is seeking to find a child, her child David. She is seeking to find her child.

Q: Explain about mist-like apparitions, balls of light, full apparitions and pure energy. Is there a protocol in these things.
A: It is learned. As you grow from a baby yourself you learn. When you go form a physical body to a spiritual body, you go through a period of learning as I have had to grow and as Elish is working on learning himself so does your spirit. Your are in a new dimension from the

physical plane and you begin to learn anew. Your learning process is not without physical form. The energy was captured at a very strong point. It takes more energy to be visible to the human eye, which is what has been seen and will continue to be seen. The strongest manifestation is in human form that they can become at that point in time. Pure energy is the natural state without being manifested in the physical plane.

Q: Why can't we capture apparitions on film, is it the frequency range of the energy fields?

A: They do not wish to be photographed. They are not ready to be seen without their physical body. When you cannot get them on film, they do not want to be captured. Yes, they can move very quickly and if they do not want to be within the range of the camera, they can be gone before you take their picture.

Q: Why can I get EMF readings then such as on the broom box in the warehouse?

A: It was not organized in its energy at that time. If they are not organized then you will not captured it on film. Let me give you an example of what I mean. If you take something and spread it very thin so you can see through it as say water. If you put a drop of water on a wooden floor and spread it with your foot, can you see it? Yet, if you put the same drop of water into a vile or test tube, can you now see it? It is basically the same with energy. When it disorganizes itself and spread itself thin you will not see it but when it bring itself into organization you will be able to see it and capture it on film.

Q: Why are spirits disorganized?
A: They do not wish to be seen or captured on film, You can pick up the energy with your meter but you will not be able to capture it on film as long as it is disorganized. Notice your photograph again and how beautifully organized the pattern is of that shape. Almost to perfection. She wanted Sharon to know she was there and that Sharon felt her and yes she did want to be seen and to let Sharon know she was there. It is also a manner of trust. A manner of not feeling violated. They are sensitive as are humans . If they are a joke or are to be scrutinized

for the reasons of making them leave. There is a difference when you approach them in that manner and the manner which you approach them at present. When they find that you are not there to harm them or do away with them then it like they are taking you in their confidences. You are going about this the proper manner.

Q: What about the spirits in our home.

A: They cannot organize themselves yet, They are too new. They do not fully understand where they are yet and their actions are sometime playful and sometimes accidental. They are not yet able to organize their energies. They are not yet strong enough and they are beginning the process of learning.

Q: How long does it take to be organized?

A: David, I cannot answer that. You must look on them as individuals as humans because they are still the essence of the person. If the person is not able to grasp quickly in life it will take longer on the other side to learn. It depends on the desires of the spirit.

December 14., 1995
Death Valley, California

Q: Do you still see the earth changes as spoken about by MGS still in the same light.

A: I think his visions are a reality but I do not see the reality of his tragedy coming immediately. There are some tremendous changes taking place on your earth and I am not certain the knowledge your people wish to gain is worth the results they achieve. They are very destructive in what they are doing. The changes are going to be progressive and you will have these changes taking place as you have seen by yourself. You have seen them now and they will not be dramatic and are taking places now as you have notice your weather patterns have changed, they have changed progressive. There will be some serious problems as a result of your scientist attempting to gain knowledge and the changes you see taking places now will progressive worsen and bring you to a point of what your futurist are seeing. The magnitude will gain intensity and the destruction will become more destructions. As you know I have no time in my world. I can tell you David, if the experimenting and testing does not desist, all it will take is one major test to set off a chain of events to cause destruction that Mr. Scallion is telling you about. If they can be controlled in the types of the things that they are doing to your world, the chances of the events can change to not be tragedy and the world can become in balance once again.

Q: Are there safe areas where we can live should this happen?

A: I have told you of one place which would be safe for you. It is not exclusive, okay. There are many places where you could be living in existence and you are looking at them at this time. You have wisdom within you and the information I relate to you is only is confirmation of what is in your heart and mind. Anywhere you go you will find those you can learn from. The weather is changing everywhere. There may be some sacrifices you have to make and a time of discomfort, anywhere you go you will find an area of discomfort. Listen to your heart and mind and to one another. The place you decide upon will be the right place for you. Get a

DAVE R. OESTER

pencil, draw a line from North to South on
your country map, try to remain along that
line. If this is of any benefit to you or give
you some comfort. The line from where I
have discussed with you from North to
South. You have these things in you
already, the only things you lack is the lack
of confidence in yourself and in each
other's. You have the wisdom within
yourself just listen to yourself, the words
are being given to you. You are being
given the answers, open your minds the
both of you.

Q: I asked questions about the health
concerning our parents.
A: It is funny the factor of death in
your race. The feelings, your emotions,
unhappiness, the despair, the loneliness is
so costly to your lives. It is amazing what
is revealed most have not believed and
dismissed and set aside. There is much
more revealed about life after life but they
do not listen. You have a tremendous
opportunity with what you are doing and
you could do some enlightening and
revealing about life after life that no other
have been able to do. You are learning for

yourselves some very important things that are happening and you don't need to fear.

Q: Questions about people who depart this life in death.

A: Your question is very good but I am not able to answer it at this time, David, on a human understanding, yes you would see a tunnel or a light. It is very hard to describe the beauty of the energy you would become. You become a part of that. They are content to remain, it is what they know, it is what they are comfortable with.

Q: Example, death is a large room within a building. You realize you are a life form and instead of continuing through the exit door they return to the earth plane from which they have arrived.

A: This is a variation of the actual experience. At times there is an urgency David, an urgency to make certain things are done within the proper way, an urgency that keeps the energy earthbound. It was urgency in life and it is the same once the physical body passes on. The emotions remain the same. The emotional urgency becomes like an energy field drawing them back preventing them from moving onward. If I might give you an example should Sharon's daughter die very suddenly. She would remain behind, her concerns would be so great for her son and her anger so great that she should remain earthbound thought she would not be a positive entity. She would be a negative entity that feeds off of other people negative energy.

Q: Is our life form the only ones to have this negative energy?

A: There are others. There are other species that have emotions David, your world is not exclusive to that.

Q: Are these other species with emotional problems who experience similar problems when they die, will they too become earthbound to their planet?

A: Yes, but I must admit it is not common. There are many worlds with life that do not have the emotional complexities of your world.

Q: If our origins were the stars, why were we inbred with these emotional seeds. Was our progenitors also with the same types of emotions.

A: Yes. The race that seeded your world was a dying people. They have not completely died out, they have to make changes there again we are getting into areas that are very difficult to explain. The time will come when you will see and understand, be assured!

Q: In your world did you have similar difficulties when you had physical bodies when the time for transition in death occurred?

A: Oh yes, you can, or maybe not at this time but the day will come when you will see, it will almost look like a pattern in a learning process, universal light. You are not the first people to destroy the life given to you. Your planet is very difficult but in learning, there is always a downfall, a consequence to experimenting with things better left alone.

February 27, 1996
Painted Rock State Park
Yuma, AZ

Sharon is doing well, but she is having a problem. She is having problem focusing as she is feeling a very strong force that you should be aware of. It is a physical pull, It is a pull to the scared things by the spirits that remain. The spirits are either positive or negative, there is a bond, a kinship there. These spirits manifested themselves to Sharon as a wolf that she observed. They wanted to let her know they were here and they knew she was here, There have been visitors who are not of this earth that have visited this general area, but not this specific site. The stone with the space helmet is a sign from another place then here. This area is proliferated with signs and tokens left behind not specifically where you have seen them, but for miles around there are places that have been visited. This site was a meeting place, a connection where decisions were made. It is a place of coming together. There is not one specific site but there are places near here that contains what you speak of for vortexes, The hot springs is not as a strong of a place as others but it is a vortex of sorts. You may find David, in your travels, that there is a lot of pain and anguish that remains behind, not specially in one area but overall. There has been a lot of pain and the spirits are not positive nor negative as you would think but they are wandering. It is difficult to give a specific answer, This was their land, this was their place. They are earthbound because of their land and what they suffered. They watch and they seek to find a peacefulness upon the land.

Noda, I had a dream about a transport stick. I saw a man in a robe but did not know him, The message was to move on. You do not need a transport stick to move onward. I will continue to show you as I promised in the past. Did you not recognize me in your dream, I will show you more, I will appear as what will make you comfortable as I do to Sharon, The knowledge you gained in small amounts will take you far. It resembles more of knowledge then did it seem to be in the dream as a transport stick. As you became more overwhelmed with what you saw, it was time for you to depart. I was able to show you a different place. The worlds you saw do exist as I showed them to you. I was wanting you to focus on where you were seeing them. You saw no sunlight, when you are told that there is no life outside earth, you will know that is not correct. Life does not have to exist on the surface. The world I shown to you is not documented by your people. These people are where you have come. They are your forefathers, David. You came from these beings, you are from them. It was more important for you to observe then to ask questions, to see all that was going around you. Why speak when you should be observing. You focus on speech not on the worlds you are on. I will take you to worlds so you can see.

The tribe that came to this site is not necessary the Hohokam. I do not wish for Sharon to have contact with the spirits here, it is not a good time for that. I don't know that their intentions are the best. I don't know that it would be good for her to talk with them. Sharon was one of the members of the tribe at the time and this is why she has a desire to learn more about the tribes. They called her by the name of KaChuKa or Lovely One. None of her current family or friends were reincarnated here. I will show her what it was like but it will be difficult for a time as I showed her daughter.

Sharon has told me of a few of the places you plan to go. I must suggest that you go with your inner feelings when you are drawn to it. You are drawn for a purpose. There are so many places it is hard to name them all.

When considering the total disregard and disrespect for the earth, earth changes are a must. You will be aware of it and yet you will not know it. You will be as you are now, with intention of doing one thing and yet the purpose is for another. You will not be thinking to yourself that something is going to happen but you will leave. You will know so deeply that the reason you go to the new place but yet you will not know openly the reason for the move. As of now, I see your mother alive at the time of the destruction. I see the earth changes as a reality but the time is the biggest factor and the time will be lengthy for the third phase. There has been a lot of land loss on your planet but it has taken a long time for the loss of the land. It has not been a very quick happening. I do not see the earth changes happening in a fast manner and not before your eyes. I see it happening in a lengthy period of time and the damage done to the land will be like erosion chipping away parts of it. It is not just the shifting and there is a lot more that will complicate the coast line and compound the problem with the experimenting with the weather changes, these factors have to be taken in serious consideration. You have seen what has happen in the area you live t this year. The changes are dramatic because of the things being done to your world. Your people are not in harmony with each other or with your planet. You are on a downhill fault.

Ghost Entities and UFO--They both reflect dimension, only the visitation from other worlds is a very higher dimension David, whereas the dimension between life after life and death is like a sheer curtain. They are similar but much difference. It is easier for them to come here inter dimensionary. When we are finish here, I would like you to get a book, hold it up to your eyes, open the cover and run your pages over the pages consider each page to be a dimension. That will give you an idea how infinite the dimension are. Dimensions from coming from other Universe to our own universe. As time go by, I will show you in dreams. I have told that when you were ready, I would show you. This is just the beginning. I want you to keep a journal of what I have been teaching you.

Noda showed Sharon that she had a little Indian baby whose hair was jet black. She was a member of this Indian tribe.

March 13, 1996
Point of the Rocks RV Park
Prescott, AZ

Q: Is there a frequency that would identify the energy patterns of ghosts?

A: I am not certain it would be in a realm you could use. I am not sure if I could help you at this time. Let me see what I can discover.

Q: The entity we encountered last night knew of you. Do many know of you.

A: We are as one, There are levels as you gain knowledge, as you grow on this side, you will find levels. The time you have with me is very valuable and you must not waste it.

Q: Is the White Mountains in Arizona that you spoke of concerning underground alien bases/secret bases. What about Secret Mountain and the man named Robert Morningsky.

A: Yes. There is a connection between Robert Morningsky and the secret bases you spoke of. The mountain area I have revealed to you is connected to what Mr. Morningsky spoke about.

Q: Is Prescott-Prescott Valley associated with UFO's?

A: There has been some curiosities concerning his area but it has not come to abduction, but rather some UFO sightings, It has not been a real active area at this time, There seems to be some curiosity about this areas that might increase activities. There are some minerals, the area is open and becoming more populated, but at this time, there is a lot open space and untouched minerals an elements. They have geological interest. The aliens are from the outer dimensions and your government is not involved here, but given time they will be. On the aliens worlds, elements have been depleted on their worlds and they seek sources here.

They need metals and natural elements. They do not come for crystals but for communications through them at such places as Sedona. There is too much that is lacking and the populous must live beneath the surface, how much do you think is available to them. Races have died, races have diminished with such minute amounts, you would be amazed yourself. It is not only the base metals but for precious metals that are needed.

April 6, 1996
Klamath Falls, OR
Regarding Interview at Rachel, Nevada
with Bruce M.

Q: Is there a frequency that might identify a ghostly entity.

A: You have learned of life after life, you have learned of disorganization, organization with intensity. With the type of range between the two, which is it you would like. The frequencies is different. When you have great strength in one, the frequency would be far greater then a weak disorganized entity. The general frequency for a organized entity with intensity is 7,783.0 hz.

Q: Yesterday, we met a young man in Rachel, NV. Is he the one you spoke of who is the Advocate?

A: Yes, when the time comes, you will be contacted. Yes.

Q: Did we spend long enough with the implant?

A: No more time was necessary, The time that was allowed was what was needed. The important thing to keep in mind is that you made contact, The decision to work with you is his, otherwise there will be others. Like you, he is impatient, he is ready to expose himself to the world and he needs to be more aware for caution where he can share with you his knowledge that is where you are to begin. You can consider putting information together as in a book, but it will take time, he is a helpful man and is given gratuity and for odd jobs. He has sufficient for his needs. He will always be as he is. He is not afforded the luxury of settling in one place for long periods of time, but he has accepted his life as it is and goes on with it. He was directed to meet you, he was there to see who and what you are. He was directed by his own kind. Of course, you know I am with you and I watch you and I also have a tendency to direct your paths upon occasion.

Q: Since his mother was barren at the time he was conceived, would he be a child of the stars? Is his father an alien?

A: You have yourself heard at various time of genetic breeding. You could say simply that he is a child of the stars. You listen to his words, listen very closely. There are things that he will not tell you directly, you will learn, you will still have the responsibility of interpreting, listen to his words.

Q: You have suggested that he has been directed by someone. Why do they want him to meet us?

A: I not certain that I can make you understand at this point, I want you to trust, call it blind faith, trust in me. If I were to guide you to a place where the culture was different, would you not want some knowledge of that culture before you got there. What you are going to attain very slowly is knowledge at this point, the more knowledge you gain, the more clear things will be to you. You must learn patience and learn to take things one step at a time. I feel you are ready for someone to work with you and teach you, what I wish you to know the knowledge that you request from me in time past. It will take a period of time, it will depend on his feelings. If he feels he can help, he will contact you. If he feels like he need a closeness, he will stay. If he feels like he needs to leave, he will need a device to record and sent that to you. If you send it to Henderson, he will receive it.

Q: Where are we heading with this knowledge? Will we be taken off world?

A: One could lead to the other, presently it is knowledge that you have requested of me. There is a great possibilities that you will be going to other worlds if you are ready at the time.

Q: Will others be going to these worlds?

A: Yes, David. Those who ask will receive what they are looking for.

Q: Would this man be considered a blue children spoken by Gordon Michael Scallion?

A: No, he is not a blue child.

Q: This young man is looking for other implants, will he find another one that he can share his life with?

A: There are many and yet they have not found each other. They will walk separate paths and not find each other, This plan for them is not of me, As you wish to gain knowledge of other worlds, other worlds wish to gain knowledge of you. They do not always have the same accessibility that you have, other worlds chose other means available. They wish to make themselves known, but they are not accessible to your people at this time.

Q: What is your relationship to these other visitors or aliens. Manny said you were a god entity, how do others look upon you?

A: Different ways. I am considered a god to all, yet other species do not know of god as you humans. I am talking of a vast amount of life and I cannot give you a one word specific answer.

Q: Does this young man know of you or his controllers?

A: He would not know of me. The life forms that work with him would only know of me if they had called for me, They are not on the same plane as I am, It is a very difficult thing to understand. There are some things that I am certain I can answer for you. There are times when I am called upon, than I am able to give direction. I have told you I would send an Advocate. As I would send you, should he need help so I sent him to you.

August 15, 1996
River Ends Campground & RV Park
Chinook, WA

Q: Do you foresee earth changes as a result of comets such as Hale Bob and the next four or five years along with another comet that is to approach.

A: Yes, they were foretold to the Native American.

Q: What happens after the transformation?

A: Renewal. A replenishing.

Q: What about the secret organization that experimenting with the weather and the existing government that is controlling human affairs?

A: Why do you think they will survive? Do you think their hiding places are so secret that they can't be taken. Do you see the people coming to terms with the corruption, being used by the government, people getting tired and angry about things that have been happening without their knowing it. You are far better to trust in your fellow man than to trust those in power.

Q: Have we followed the focus you suggested to us before.

A: You have become focus on what you are doing, you are back on the path. Do not put all your dreams and hopes in one place as you will limit your own ability and dreams, but you must be aware of what you have around you and the possibilities of what could occur if you just hold on to your one dream, you could be so focus on your future that the life around you could crumble without you seeing what is happening. If your relationship remains strong and secure, but your security is wavering a bite, make certain that you can maintain what you have.

Q: Do you have any closing messages for Sharon and myself?

A: You are growing together as one which I am very happy to see the barriers beginning to come down you will need each other in the future and it is good to see the bonding between you. I just want to say thank you for consulting with me and to allow me to watch these changes in your growth taking place at a later time I will talk with you again. My best to you David.

December 6, 1997
Beverly Beach State Park, Oregon

I have been observing and what I am hearing and seeing, I am not certain I am able to find the word to describe to you. I do not think you are going in the wrong direction, but your people have taken some wrong turns, it saddens us to see what is taking place. You are seeing the same thing and feeling the same thing, you're feeling the same for what we have observed from here. There is a lot of unrest and uncertainty.

Then what I have told you has been proven to you, has it not? (Millennial Madness) You have a wonderful tool (Internet) available and you are putting it to very good use. You are doing very well, you should be proud of your effect and your successes. You are touching many lives, it is easy for your kind to be carried away with a negative, paranoid thoughts and feelings, panic will result and nothing good can come from these things, but to have those who can reason and use this to calm the spirits of those confused is very important and you have used your tool very well.

Since our last conversation, you have expanded into many areas. I knew it would come about, you have taken what has been given to you and used it wisely. It will continually to be this way. The path you are on is the right one as long as you stay on this path you will find yourself expanding from where you are even now and you are wise to use what is available to you to reach out to help those who have confidences and trust in your ability and wisdom. As you grow, you will know the directions to take. There is a great deal of respect and admiration for the job you are doing and you will continue to do this well as you are growing.

The Tornado Lamps are a good example of from disorganization to organization. What begins as a single cell grows to become what you are now, which is organized cellular structure and in relationships to balls of light they organize themselves to become what you are finding on your film, a single ball of light which can contain many balls of light, be it vortex which as you watch your lamp you will see it changing from a disorganized state to an organized tornado shape or be it any other form that you capture on film. It is an organized state.

You can represent yourself as a single ball of light or in combination with balls of light in a single state. You have been given examples of balls of light that have separated. There has been incidences where this has been more than one, two spirits. There is no limitation. The only limitation is in the minds of your people. But your people are very limited in their thinking, you must allow yourselves to imagine any possibility. There are more possibility available then once you leave this physical plane then you are allowing yourself to imagine.

A vortex may represent hundreds of spirit entities or one spirit entity. The reasons spirits join together is because when you pass into the other realm you will find you are surrounded with those you have been intrigued with, curious, you will find that you are with your kind and you will find yourselves together.

And if there were physical bodies in one place, more than one physical body they would naturally want to return to that place, not singularly but collectively. (The five fingers on a hand coming together to represent the hand example).

The tornado shape is a process of moving, one of the many. You have yet a lot to learn of these things. It is also a means of indicating to you that there is something very present there. Would you be prepared on a darkened stairway to see the full figure of a human form?

This vortex is something that you have been able to reveal and look at the interest it has generated. (What determine the size and brightness of the balls of light?) They represent different levels of energy. The very strong will show themselves more obviously to you. The energy level is determined in part by how long the entity has been here in this world and the strength of the individual spirit. It is the conditions surrounding the spirit at the time it appears. Your earth condition contributes a lot. Do you recall as we walked together in that cemetery. And do you recall the storm, and do you remember what you could visualize. Here the experience was a unique one, the voice that was heard, the balls of light there was a lot that you were able to experience due to the conditions.

The times of a storm is good, the spirits are strongest during the full or new time, or the time of the full or new moon. It is best when there is an electromagnetic activity, it does not have to be a powerful storm with lightning strikes but the air itself is charged which is conducive to these energies not manifesting themselves to you. Low or high pressure zones is not important, but the storm itself.

(Note: What I was calling a vortex was later updated to an "orb in motion that is leaving a contrail behind it.")

Old cemeteries are access ports to the other dimensions for spirits to enter and depart our world. It is one strong area: Youngs Falls is one such vortex area:

In regards to very negative energy entities, there are many difficult circumstances as there are many surrounding conditions that must be taken into consideration. First of all, you speak to them of the history. If the land has had violent acts you know the scenario for negative haunting. Negativity in the home, feeding on the fear, feeding on the negative it is as though certain criteria is meet. The haunting will be of a negative nature. When changes are made be it strength, be it a lack of fear, setting fear aside and being strong against the presence that is negative. If you can change the element the entity is feeding on then there will not be the malevolent activity. But as long as the elements are there for that kind of atmosphere it will be something to continue. What you are telling those who contact you in regards to anger and negative energy is very correct. One needs to look closely at the individual elements involved, the individual people involved and there are certain natural things that can be done to minimize the activity. To alleviate the activity one needs to change the patterns within themselves, The only way to remove a negative haunting is to change the human behavior that allows the entity to feed within the haunting.

Possession by negative spirits is very rare. You must consider that you do not hear of openly. These are rare situation that do occur every once in a while. They do occur but it is very rare.

You must remember that when you are getting together with other people to speak, these people are children; these people are just beginning to learn so you must start with the basic steps. As you grow and as you learn you will be able to put into words the teachings I give to you.

As you are building your business, begin setting aside whatever you can for your future move.

You must understand that to help the spirits you must be close to them, in seaside you were able to help a small child. She communicated with you and she was ready to go and find her mother. She was in direct contact with you. That is not always possible as you are finding out, but be aware David, that what you hear may not have the same meaning to you as it does to the source.

You have a purpose, you must understand that not all spirits are condemned to remain here. ALL spirits can return at will. It is not just a few. Your father awaits your mother and he comes to see that she is okay at will, at his will. Other family members do the same. Jim returns at will, did he not tell you. The spirit of anyone can return at will it does not necessary mean that they have to remain here to be earth bound. Yes there are those who have anchors that keep them here, but overall the spirits of the departed loved ones return at will.

Your purpose is to observe yourselves and share that knowledge that there is life after physical life that there is no need to fear passing from this physical life, there is no reason to fear the presence of a spirit. The spirit is the spirit of a human like meeting someone on the street who is a stranger but has much to share and there is no reason to fear. They only lack a physical body. Learning from your ancestors can give you great insights, learning from the presence=s can give you greater insights into life after this life and your purpose is to learn and to share, to help, to reach out and eliminate the fear that is so senseless. To bring those together who wish to know more and to understand what it is that awaits you all.

Communication with spirits: It is like wanting to speak to someone who does not speak your language, yes there is a desire to speak, to communicate but until one or the other learns the language there is very little communication and to truly to communicate with spirits require knowledge and growth. There are few who are prepared to do this. Do not encourage people to do this prematurely. When they are ready the ability will be there for them, but until then they are not ready for it.

Light Beings at Devils Tower: There are those which are of the light beings that are like the balls of light, you are correct. There have been times when the Light Beings have come through the portal in cemeteries. The Light Beings may not be distinguish between Balls of Light. The ships are spheres or ball shaped.

You need available to you a program that is strongest enough to determine the differences between the Light Beings and the Balls of Light and could determine between them.

What I have told you in the past holds true.

April 30, 1998
KOA Campground, Astoria, OR

Q: What do the colors represent in orbs?

A: The colors have nothing special to represent.

Q: What do the various shapes of orbs represent?

A: No, as you have people of people of different sizes and different shapes and different colors it is the same. On the next plane, you have spoken of different forms of life after life, as to animals, some of these are the animals you speak of as well as those who pass beyond.

Q: Do all life forms have orb forms? What about insects such as bees?

A: No, bees and insects do not come back. It is higher forms of life, which come back in the form of energy as you have seen and as you have learned.

Q: What constitute a higher life form?

A: Ones that have the senses similar to humans, the keen senses, the ability to feel as well. The higher life form is what constitute the life form, the emotional energy into which this goes to form your spirit which is what goes on from this life.

Q: What does the those photos that show hundreds of energy plasma orbs within a single larger orb?

A: In your world as in most, smaller parts create a larger form. If I can help by explaining to you a person become married to another, this become the beginning of a family. Children are added and the family grows and become bigger and becomes part of the community becomes a part of the overall community of state, each step by step the smaller part become a part of the whole and this is what you are seeing. Yes, there are forms of life, the orbs within the whole and most often you do not see this but at times you will, but what you are seeing is small parts of energy that are forming a larger overall energy, almost like a community would be to you.

Q: What would this larger energy community represent?

A: In part for companionship, you have seen how the energy will cling to a life, the living around you. This is a form you are seeing of moving on, a collective energy in such a form, of similar to getting on a bus, similar to that type of movement, of moving on. The collective energy is like a transport vehicle. It is like a magnet with draws these things together to move on.

This collective energy pattern made up of hundreds of orbs is used to enter or leave our realm. Generally yes, but you must understand there are circumstances where this is not the case always. It is a form of moving, a form of more energy to move from place to place, from this realm to the next or from the next realm to this. You also have areas on your earth that are more energized with this life after life. If you had captured such anomalies in Gettysburg than you could not say it was a form of transportation necessary from one realm to the next realm because of the energy there, but this is collective energy that overall remain in the same place, but not really leaving, but moving from area to area, but David more or less anchored.

Q: Are energy spheres that contain many anomalies in cemeteries the energy portals to transport spirits?
A: Yes.

Q: Would these energy patterns resemble an orb instead of a vortex when used as a portal?
A: Do you not have on your plane a mass of EM energy as you have been

hearing of in areas where the weather has been terribly bad. What do you see the energy pattern doing, what do you see happening.

(Dave) Many times you see tornados forming.

(Noda) Exactly that. You also must remember that you still have a great deal to learn and still as humans have a tendency to limit your thinking. Thorough you are very open minded, mind you, overall the possibility is enormous. Am I clear? There are many different forms of transports available, such as collective sphere and vortices. As you progress you are finding more than you were before, You spoke of colors and shapes. Think back to your first photograph and look at what you are coming to, what you are finding now and you will find more as you are ready for it. You will find more different from one you are getting now and you will begin to see more of a pattern to what you find.

Q: Is there any way to determine now what is an animal spirit and what is a human spirit?

A: There are two possible it is difficult to determine. For animal spirits, look for small bright orbs which move very quickly and at times they can be very faint, but it very difficult, there is no standard to go by. You need to find a pet cemetery, a place where there were only animals. For humans, look for larger orbs. It is generally the case there is no standard by which you can go, you can only compare what you are getting and coming to our own conclusion, you are very good at that.

Q: What about Shad's grave and the orbs?

A: She is not alone. There are several that can be with her. There are three which were previously pets associated Sharon. There is also one which was associated with you. (Misty) She does not come frequently, but she does come, she is very content and she is very happy where she is. The gray cat can see shadow and her friends when they come. There is also other cats there before, the cats are buried in the area and have stayed. Some may have lived there. The gray cat likes shadow and finds it warm where Shad is buried,

Q: Why are digital cameras able to capture the orbs that film cameras miss?

A: David, I am not certain what the orb with a bullseye in it is, it could be an artificial anomaly. Possibility you are capturing a light being, I find it somewhat difficult to. There is not a lot of difference, David, there is some similarities yet there are some distinct difference.

May I ask you, is it similar to the large bubble like structure that you describe earlier.

(Note: The bullseye in an orb simply means it is an airborne dust particle.)

(Dave) No

(Noda) Generally there would be more than one to be a Light Being. They would be photographed higher than what you are seeing closer to the ground, such as in your Gettysburg and in battlefield cemetery. They (Light Beings) would be higher, brighter, multiple, with distinct edges. Shield design are a different formation of energy that you are trying to discover. These shields are generally human spirits.

(Noda) I have shown her a part of my city, I have showed her what you call my token, my symbol. I have shown her on my plane of existence when life was abundance that our cities were underground and I have shown her the purity that you will find when you will join me upon your death and you both will be with me in your coming and going. We will meet.

Q: Concerns about money and our move.

A: I do not see that you will draw the interest here that you have on the Eastern part of the country, there is just a newness here, a religious domination. It is very difficult to explain, but you do not have the same desires as back east, What limits here is not limiting back East,

Q: I am having dreams about my Dad.

A: He is not able to reach your mother, he is not able to make his presence known to her. When he is she is still not accepting of him coming to him and she puts it out of her mind and when you ask, she does not recall. He comes to you and you are open and receptive of him where she is not. It is still a very difficult thing for her to deal with as she is not able to speak of him openly, she holds in her feelings.

Q: Who was the woman in the dream?

A: I am not certain, but it may have been his mother when she was young, There are reasons he is present in your dreams. One of the reason is to make yourself aware of his presence and the second is to let you know that he is prepared to accept your mother when she is ready but he can't show himself to her presently. It is a way of preparing you as well because of what I have told you.

Q: Does he know it is getting close to when she will pass over?

A: Yes, that is part of his purpose of preparing us. He does try to prepare Steve, who has dreamt of him, but not as often. You are the one. He has not spoken to you, yet he know he wishing to tell you something and he will convey his message to you when the time is near and right. Ask your Dad to let you know when it time for your Mom to cross over.

June 20,1998
KOA Campground, Madras, OR

Q: Gordon Michael Scallion, Ed Dames and Hopi Elders all related same substance for graphic changes to the Earth.

A: I foresee changes taking place as I have told you in the past.

Q: Is it speeding up?

A: I do not see that taking place not to the severity of what you are being told.

Q: What about harmful Solar radiation being emitted to the earth?

A: I see the changes taking place within your solar system and yet I cannot confirm to you what they are telling you and I do not really see it David.

Q: You're saying changes in weather patterns will continue to happen but the severity of earth changes that will take approximately one third of human life as forecasted will not happen?

A: I see the weather changing dramatically from what it has been happening. There are changes that will be taking place but they have they have not been accelerated. However the progress continues. A lot of what you are being told there is a connection between these who see into the future and yet you must understand they come from a common source. The source is to bring your people to a place which will cause them enough fear to make change for the betterment of our world.

Q: Is that betterment to bring the people together as one people, one family and one earthling?

A: If you have one man and I will use this as an example due to your recent experience, who is laying track for a railroad will it not take him far longer than if you have a team of men laying track for the railroad. You are each in the process of going individual ways without concerns for one another. It is not only the selfishness of individual who is devastating your planet. Your people have a strange fascination with power and when this becomes the focal point all, can be lost. Just remember that a great deal of what you are hearing is to instill fear enough for people to want to make change within themselves. You are evolving other people into spiritual beings, you are coming to an awareness and it is very important because you are spiritual beings but it is a slow process for your people, very slow.

Q: What is the source of information that Ed Dames and his remote viewers access for these doomsday events?

A: It is a far higher power than what you know of. You are one small part of a far greater picture. There is so much that your people is grasping for and so much knowledge that it is so far beyond their ability to understand and comprehend, but rather than taking it a step at a time as this is the manner in which your people learn, you are jumping in so many direction that you are learning very little. The source is revealing what direction you are going. The only way that your people seem to make change is when they are put in a position of fear. Is that about right? But act immediately, but what better way to get your attention than to reveal visions of things to come should change not take place, it is not too late, but the change needs to be now and they are all correct saying the same things, you need to make these changes as a people,

Q: Why is this source using fear instead of the truth to motivate people, I would expect the source to be someone like Jesus?

A: How would you go about accomplishing something of such a vast problem, how would you do it?

(Dave) Bible concepts & Jesus Christ

(Noda) But as you can see yourself, there are many more are not finding what they are searching for from within that background. You also have to understand this fact, David, that these people have had these vision and yes, they are convinced themselves of the things taking place. The fear is coming from within them which is generating fear for all, but the common goal is the same. When one have tried all avenues to reach out and touch those you might even call it a type of rehabilitation and it comes to a point when they are no longer are listening and then it has to come from something that shakes the foundations when you can have a catastrophic event take place and watch the people help people and they are back to where they were so many years ago. Why does it take an earthquake to make a neighbor to realize he has a neighbor. You have found a path that leads only to destruction, your people, your world, and the corrections has to be made as soon as possible.

Q: Noda, you are a God-Entity how are you involved with this source?

A: Yes, I am of that level but there are those above me as well. Let me tell you this before you proceed, when I speak of a higher source, I can only describe this to you as an accumulation of energies.

(Dave) Not as an entity, but as a collective consciousness.

(Noda) Yes, I am a part of that consciousness. I have been given a place where I come when I am called upon and reveal information that I can help to those who wish to evolve to a high level of understanding. A collection of rather than individual forms. It is a consciousness of ALL, of everything which is still a bit more than I feel you are ready for and yet I think it is time for you to know of more. I know your heart, do not think of me as you do (As a God), keep thinking of me as a spirit of someone who cares very deeply and wishes to help. As you said, I am a little old man in a robe, which is just the way I appear to Sharon. She finds love in that and I do not wish to be anything more frightening or intimating to her, our communications are very important as we speak thou I watch you as we speak, I am able to determine the pattern of growth that you are taking. Our visits are very important and I cherish the time we speak,

Q: My alien dreams.

A: Some I stimulate but for the purpose of showing you intelligent life in preparation for the future, you see technology of things you do not understand, one day it will come clear. You do need to be aware of the future. It is a way of preparing you. Do not be frightened of them. What you focus on what the most is what you are learning about. What I am showing is what you are not focus on, does that make sense. These are not constant in your mind, David, are they? The things you see and remember are those that you are supposed to remember, they will have a purpose in the future.

You still have a life. You two still have a life outside of your business partnership, yet I see very little laugher between you. I am certain when you are moved away the area you are in, you are still young people. You should be laughing and loving. When your people cease to laugh and enjoy a lighter side of life, the spirit begins to dim and the spirit begins to die. It is a very important part of keeping your spirit alive. You know what the balance of life means and yet there is still a lack of balance. What is it that you feel?

Take to heart what you have heard and yet understand that it is magnified in this context. You will be safe as long you take the same precautions that you would take if you were not being conditioned by fear. I know your concerns and it goes deep. You use the same judgment, for your self-preservation, you certain do understand, there are dangers and yet if you are cautious there is no worry of encounters.

Q: Did Sharon ask you about your totem?

A: There are no secrets between the three of us. I must tell you that I have many symbols, which represent myself and the things I do, but the thing that would probably stand out in one's mind the most is what I show her are of the clearest diamond quality on your earth crystal. I have done this in the past, she has had difficulties staying with me, but I show her the crystals that are almost hypnotic in nature.

Q: You don't see a need to live underground for protection.

A: No, I feel that if you find the shelter from.

December 23, 1999
La Pine State Park, OR

Q: What do you see for Y2K and the New Year?

A: Yes, there will a few things that occur out of the ordinary but overall there is no need for concern. You are doing what you need to do, you are prepared with food, are you not? Prepare yourself with water David, but aside from that it is like every new century the fears are unwarranted.

Q: What about changes in our Government?

A: No, a lot of deceit. When you have deceit, it gradually crumble. With what has taken place with your President and those around him is weakening.

Q: How should we approach this new year?

A: Remember that love is the strongest bond of all, stronger the bond, the stronger the love and the stronger the team, don't lose sight of the importance of each other, the bond that she has for you and you for her you will begin to grow in ways that you didn't expect.

Q: White Ectoplasm by shed?
A: It was natural.

Q: Fragrance at home by spirit?
A: Yes, it is a spirit. She is not related, it is not John's mother, but a spirit that finds great joy in disturbing things to let you know she is around. She did the wallet things. There are at times spirits outside of

the normal spirit that is there. You do get visitations from spirits who were regulars from the Warren house. A spirit is more of a negative nature. His knowledge of you comes to us.

Q: Will she ever show herself as an apparition?

A: No, she is not strong enough as a spirit. But as time goes by she does wish to show herself to you. The aroma you smell and the French Vanilla is used by her. She prefers your creamer. It is her humor that she enjoys with you. Her name is Linn and she is younger, twenty-eight years. She died from an illness, She is content to remain here, John was very frightened by her. He saw her in the window, She has made the small bedroom as her own, as her room. She has her own furniture and our boxes does not manner to her. Her room is very lovely as well. At times the veil is very thin. It also has to do with the world, the desire of the spirits. She wears a white dress and is a Native American but her skin is very fair. She is not from the Warm Spring Reservation. Let her know you enjoy her presence, her fragrance, her breeze you feel when she passes. It would help with the relationship. You both are very aware, but she seem to find it more humorous with your possessions. She enjoys making games in spooking you, in her random acts. She is a happy and content, when you are there, she feels accepted.

August 26, 2001
Rawlins, Wyoming
Western Hills Campground

Q: Is there a better way to express the Language of Prayer than what we have done thus far?

A: I think as you work to finish your composition that you will find the words. You are going in the right direction. You have gained much. That is good David because learning never ends.

Q: Has others gained the same insights as I have when reading the Harry Potter's books?

A: Not in the way you did. You were able to gain much from what you would call fantasy and yet the reality of it was before you and you saw that.

Q: We want to thank you from help in avoiding the two drivers who nearly crashed into us.

A: I am never far from you. The work you have before you is important. It is so essential that you take the time to prepare and get the work done, but it also time that you realize there is a need for a human to break away from the work and clear the mind and then return and you are doing well and do not worry David. It is coming along well in its own time. So do not worry.

Q: Maybe it is not so much worry as it is urgency to get the work done.

A: Were it not for the work you have already done and being known, your work would mean very little, but working to bring this information to human kind. They know that you are honest and straight forward and your work will mean much. I would like to tell you that your work will mean more as time goes by. It is not premature, the need is there, it is whether people are willing to accept and they are getting closer as they realize what they believe in is not as it has been presented to them and as time goes by, your words will mean much to more who are more willing to open themselves to the truth as you are presenting it.

Q: It almost sounds contradictory teaching about the scientific approach to ghosts and then talking about the Magic Language of Prayer.

A: You are dealing with two areas of your own world that are very conflicting. Your science is manmade. From them guidelines to follow to learn at times too strictly are these scientific approaches now with and it is important to be respected for the work you do by following scientific guidelines. On the other hand, what you are trying to do with the book is to help people come to an understanding that they are more than just sheep. There is far more to them if they believe in themselves and believe in their words and believe in their desires that can come to them and be theirs. That they can heal themselves. If people do not believe in these things they have been taught the contrary. The knowledge has been lost. You are working in two areas that are very important for mankind to survive.

Q: Are Poltergeist really another dimension, entities in another dimension that is overlapping into our dimension so we can hear them, but not be able to see them? Are ghosts simply existing in another dimension, as citizens of that dimension, evolving from our dimension and passing into another dimension?

A: You have gone far. The veil is very thin David between the physical life and the spiritual life.

Q: Is not the spiritual life, just another dimension that we call spiritual?

A: Yes.

Q: It seems to me that those dimensions overlap into our dimension when there is an increase in the geomagnetic fields caused by lunar cycles of full and new moons or by solar storms.

A: The activity within our planet can create conditions that allow the veil to become thinner.

Q: What type of activities?

A: Geomagnetic in nature David.

Q: Are there other fields other than the geomagnetic fields that affect the overlapping?

A: No.

Q: So the prime motivators are the lunar cycles and the solar storms.

A: Yes and presently they are more active than before and you are seeing and hearing more of this activity.

Q: Would this be directly related to sun spot activity?

A: Yes it would, You have factors that influence the physical body, the condition of the physical body because of its makeup. Whatever is happening, the influence, the condition of the physical body will also influence those things that are unnatural.

Q: As we see apparitions, are the other dimensions overlapping into ours also experiencing the same lunar or solar cycles as ours?

A: No. The one closest to you. Your geomagnetic and electromagnetic activity when it intensify will affect the dimensions closest to you.

Q: And those dimensions closest to us, would they be the spirits of the dead?

A: Yes David.

Q: What about the infinite multiple outcomes that exist at any given moment that we can select to displace our existing one with the new one. How are those parallel dimensions related to the dimension where the spirits of the dead are at?

A: That is knowledge far beyond what I can give you as there is so much more to that then just shifting.

Q: Can you give me some examples?

A: That is very difficult to answer.

Q: Does it have to do with the Observer Effect? The cloud of possibilities until a choice is made?

A: David, I am not certain about this. I am not understanding what this is really. You speak of past, present and future?

Q: No, I am speaking of future possibilities. For example, if I had a tumor and I visualized an outcome that did not have a tumor in it.

A: The dimension is a mirror image of you, the other side of you.

Q: Then that is what time travel is about, of position oneself in a dimension that is in the past or future.

A: Yes.

Q: Are there specific areas for us to seek out the knowledge we need?

A: Where you find comfort, where you find peace, where you can go within yourself. This place has done well for you. (Rawlins, WY) Your work is important and it is destined to be done. The book will come out well David, it will do well.

Q: I was thinking of sending off my novel, *The Prophecy*, to be published now.

A: When it is time, you will know it. It will give you peace and rest within yourself to finish it, then it is time. You must prioritize your books so you do not over realm yourself. The focus right now needs to be on finishing of the Language of Prayer because there is still keys you need to add to the book that you need to be looking for those you don't want it to end up being mediocre. You are doing something very special and it needs to be presented in a very special way and I fear it could lose the complete message with other things that are taking place and the desires you each have of prioritize what you are doing. I think your book, novel, will come out and be enjoyed by many, however, for now I think you might want to consider setting it aside.

Q: When we did the Wicca, we knew someone who practiced it, with pagan witchcraft. For the Red Road, we knew someone who practice it so we could learn the similarities and differences between it. With Nature, I am at a loss as to how to obtain the information.

A: Look within the nature of people.

Q: So looking at cities with intense negative energy verses places with positive energy.

A: That is a part of what you will learn.

Q: I had a dream about two graves, a man and a woman.

A: I think it was given to you as a message. I think it more as your mother's brother and your mother. There is going to be a time when you both have a great deal of loss, the ages of your parents are close, their health is poor. It will be time of when you will need the strength of one another to get through what is ahead. There will be great financial rewards for you both, but it is going to be a very difficult time and that is going to come in a frequent way (wave).

Q: I had a dream about meaning a son who was not born in this life, but I met him in another dimension when he asked me for advice.
A: That is right.

Q: Why did he seek me out?
A: You are his father!

Q: What about his father in his dimension?
A: It is not quite as you are thinking. It is not quite like what you are thinking David. In that you had not seen him before, you knew who he was when you spoke with Shari, is that not correct? The purpose of you and Sharon being together

is far greater than either one of you realizes. It is a cosmic thing, a cosmic relationship. You two didn't just meet randomly, the purpose of being together is a team work. I am putting emphases on the two of you because the work you do is essential for the two parts to work together. You're the right hand, her the left hand. You clasp your hands together and what do you have? A union with your knowledge which is so different from her knowledge. There is much work for you to do. There is much to teach. You are on the beginning steps of your life, your purpose and you have come so far and I am so proud to call you friend and to counsel you.

Q: Will one day we step beyond the ghost organization and teach something else?

A: You will find David that it is all the same. It is all a part of the same. It is a very complex world you live in and many questions I don't have words to explain to you because of the complexity. I don't have outright answers for you that are not far beyond your understanding, even though you are progressing in your knowledge there is still so much beyond your knowledge it would take more than one life time to learn it all, but there are some things that I cannot explain to you.

Q: That is okay, we may yet figure some of it out.

A: If you remain on the path that you are on, you will discover far more than you ever imagined. You already have, but there is so much more for you out there.

Q: So after this book, there will be more books for us to do in related areas?

A: There are more books for you to do, there are more stories for you to share. It is important to share the stories. Ghost stories and stories of those see beyond the veil between this dimension and the next. There is so much more for you to share, but I must part now. I won't be far.

January 10, 2006
Fluorite Mine
Deming, NM

Q: Sharon has concerns about the area we are camped in with blockages of energy flow.

A: There is much that is blocking her energy at the moment and you must be aware of the things surround her. It seems that you are drifting from the place where you should be.

Q: And where is that Noda?

A: There is much to learn, I have much to teach you. It is the energies outside of you that is taking you from the place you need to be.

Q: Is there a better place for us be camped for a while that has better energies?

A: Where you are there will be energies that are not to your benefit and the focus is lost. I can be with you but you cannot reach me because of energies coming in your direction. At times, you are blocked and you are surrounded by a negative energy sent to you which it prohibits anything it so subtle yet you find you accomplish nothing in your endeavors. We will speak many times as you call upon me, I am with you wherever you go. I try to inform and help you, but you must listen closely to your heart, to the voice within you for it is me many times.

Q: Who is sending this negative energies?

A: There are many David.

Q: Is it from the living or the dead?

A: The living, who see you as threats to them.

(Note: At this time we were getting death threats and hate mail from fans of a TV ghost hunting show. Apparently the leaders were jealous of us and encouraged their members to send us hate mail and this was the source of the negative energy that was being sent to us. We took steps to block this negative energy and was successful at blocking this negativity.)

IN CONCLUSION

This book has been very difficult for me because Noda's words meant so much to us over the years. When I look back on what Noda told me concerning the earth changes when all of the well-known futurists and doomsday slayers were forecasting catastrophic changes I am amazed.

Noda told me that these doomsday slayers were not accurate in their forecasting. He said look back at the last thousand years and see how the earth has changed and it will be the same now. He was right. So many times he told us information that proved to be very accurate.

I was also shy about revealing Noda to the public and that Sharon Gill Oester was a gifted trance medium channeler. When I shared with Susan Olson that Sharon was a trance medium channeler and that she had channeled Noda for fifteen years, Susan also tried to talk to Noda. She succeeded and then told me that she had also talked to my late wife Sharon and that I should share Noda's teachings in a book.

I thought about it and am taking the risk of being laughed at since I have always relied on scientific tools to document the existence of the spirits of the dead.

Just so you know, I have not been able to channel Noda, my mind would never quiet down so I could go into a trance state. I wish I could trance Noda, I miss him since Sharon has passed over to the beautiful Afterlife where she having the time of her life now.

I want the readers of this book to know that I still hold my friendship with Noda as a sacred relationship. I was told countless times that I was trying to learn too fast and I needed to slow down as I was not capable of comprehending the answers to some of my questions I would ask Noda.

Noda taught me about unconditional love that I have never experienced in the past. At times I was put on the spot by Noda for asking too many questions that I was not ready to understand.

I have left out Noda's comments that were too personal to Sharon or myself to share in this book. Noda also gave me over 150 different healing rates for healing the human body. The healing rates Noda gave me worked time and again.

Forgive any grammar errors found in this book, Noda did the best he could at describing what he wanted us to know, but often times, his grammar was far from perfect, especially coming from an alien spirit guide.

Anyone who can channel, I would suggest they ask for Noda and he will come to you. He never forces himself onto anyone, but he will respond to a call to him. Yes, he is an alien spirit guide, but he always will appear as a kind loving person, he is never scary or looking like a Hollywood monster portrayed in films about aliens.

Whether you trance mentally or allow Noda to use your voice box, he will come to you. Remember, Noda said, "My purpose is to assist those who request my help."

In Sharon's case, when she channeled, Noda would take her to a cliff overlooking a beautiful ocean or to the beautiful Crystal City with gigantic vertical crystals. Sharon always felt very secure and safe when she was with Noda.

We both knew that Noda loved us and was watching out for us. At times, he intervened and saved us from accidents when a driver would run the red light and would have T-boned us, but we were miraculously saved from death.

If you do channel Noda, please drop me an email to ghostwebe@ghostweb.com and share your experience. I would appreciate it very much. Thank you.

Dave R. Oester
Kingman, AZ
October 2014

ABOUT THE AUTHOR

Dave Oester, DD., Ph.D., and Reiki Master is an ordain and licensed metaphysical minister focusing on the eternal nature of man. He has been sharing NODA's teachings since 1996 through his web site at www.ghostweb.com. Dr. Oester has worn many hats in his life. He was a geophysical oil consultant, owned and operated an oil drilling company, worked as a treasure hunter, an accountant, a paralegal, and as the head of the International Ghost Hunters Society since 1996. He operates a small book publishing business called Coyote Moon Publishing. He has been writing books since 1992. He now has sixty-three books published including eighteen novels. You can contact him at dave@ghostweb.com.